Goodness Gracious Me!

AUTHORS

ELAINE MEI AOKI
VIRGINIA A. ARNOLD
JAMES FLOOD
JAMES V. HOFFMAN
DIANE LAPP
MIRIAM MARTINEZ

ANNEMARIE SULLIVAN
 PALINCSAR
MICHAEL PRIESTLEY
NANCY ROSER
CARL B. SMITH

WILLIAM H. TEALE
JOSEFINA VILLAMIL
 TINAJERO
ARNOLD W. WEBB
PEGGY E. WILLIAMS
KAREN D. WOOD

MACMILLAN/McGRAW-HILL SCHOOL PUBLISHING COMPANY

NEW YORK   CHICAGO   COLUMBUS

AUTHORS, CONSULTANTS, AND REVIEWERS

WRITE IDEA! Authors

Elaine Mei Aoki, James Flood, James V. Hoffman, Diane Lapp, Ana Huerta Macias, Miriam Martinez, Ann McCallum, Michael Priestley, Nancy Roser, Carl B. Smith, William Strong, William H. Teale, Charles Temple, Josefina Villarnil Tinajero, Arnold W. Webb, Peggy E. Williams

The approach to writing in Macmillan/McGraw-Hill Reading/Language Arts is based on the strategies and approaches to composition and conventions of language in Macmillan/McGraw-Hill's writing-centered language arts program, WRITE IDEA!

Multicultural and Educational Consultants

Alma Flor Ada, Yvonne Beamer, Joyce Buckner, Helen Gillotte, Cheryl Hudson, Narcita Medina, Lorraine Monroe, James R. Murphy, Sylvia Pena, Joseph B. Rubin, Ramon Santiago, Cliff Trafzer, Hai Tran, Esther Lee Yao

Literature Consultants

Ashley Bryan, Joan I. Glazer, Paul Janeczko, Margaret H. Lippert

International Consultants

Edward B. Adams, Barbara Johnson, Raymond L. Marshall

Music and Audio Consultants

John Farrell, Marilyn C. Davidson, Vincent Lawrence, Sarah Pirtle, Susan R. Snyder, Rick and Deborah Witkowski

Teacher Reviewers

Terry Baker, Jane Bauer, James Bedi, Nora Bickel, Vernell Bowen, Donald Cason, Jean Chaney, Carolyn Clark, Alan Cox, Kathryn DesCarpentrie, Carol L. Ellis, Roberta Gale, Brenda Huffman, Erma Inscore, Sharon Kidwell, Elizabeth Love, Isabel Marcus, Elaine McCraney, Michelle Moraros, Earlene Parr, Dr. Richard Potts, Jeanette Pulliam, Michael Rubin, Henrietta Sakamaki, Kathleen Cultron Sanders, Belinda Snow, Dr. Jane Steubing, Margaret Mary Sulentic, Barbara Tate, Seretta Vincent, Willard Waite, Barbara Wilson, Veronica York

ACKNOWLEDGMENTS

The publisher gratefully acknowledges permission to reprint the following copyrighted material:

"Coco Can't Wait!" originally published under the title "Hayaku Aitaina" by Taro Gomi. Copyright © 1979 by Taro Gomi. English translation rights arranged with Ehonkan Co. Ltd. through Japan Foreign-Rights Centre. Used by permission of Japan Foreign-Rights Centre.

"Hattie and the Fox" is the entire text and all artwork from HATTIE AND THE FOX by Mem Fox. Copyright © 1986 by Mem Fox. Reprinted with permission from Bradbury Press, an affiliate of Macmillan, Inc.

"I Need a Lunch Box" is the entire text and art from I NEED A LUNCH BOX by Jeannette Caines. Illustrated by Pat Cummings. Text copyright © 1988 by Jeannette Caines. Illustrations copyright © 1988 by Pat Cummings. Reprinted by permission of HarperCollins Publishers.

"Robert, Who Is Often a Stranger to Himself" from BRONZEVILLE BOYS AND GIRLS by Gwendolyn Brooks. Copyright © 1956 by Gwendolyn Brooks Blakely. Reprinted by permission of HarperCollins Publishers.

"Something Big Has Been Here" from SOMETHING BIG HAS BEEN HERE by Jack Prelutsky. Text copyright © 1990 by Jack Prelutsky. Reprinted by permission of Greenwillow Books, a division of William Morrow and Company, Inc., Publishers, New York.

"The Folk Who Live in Backward Town" from HELLO AND GOOD-BY by Mary Ann Hoberman. Copyright © 1959, renewed 1987 by Mary Ann Hoberman. Reprinted by permission of Gina Maccoby Literary Agency.

"The Story of Chicken Licken" by Jan Ormerod. Copyright © 1985 by Jan Ormerod. By permission of Lothrop, Lee & Shepard, a division of William Morrow and Company, Inc., Publishers, New York.

COVER DESIGN: WYD Design
COVER ILLUSTRATION: Kenneth Spengler

DESIGN CREDITS
WYD Design, 6-9, 42-43
Designframe Incorporated, 80-81

ILLUSTRATION CREDITS
Marty Norman, 6-9; Roger Beerworth, 42-43; Anna Walker, 44-45; Jayne Holsinger, 142-143.

PHOTOGRAPHY CREDITS
All photographs are by the Macmillan/McGraw-Hill School Division (MMSD) except as noted below.
10: Courtesy of Japan Foreign Rights Centre. 42:t.l. Cindy Lewis, t.r. Bette S. Garber/Highway Images; b.l. Chris Jones/The Stock Market; b.r. Bob Abraham/The Stock Market. 43: t. Robert Semeniuk/The Stock Market; b.l. Joe Towers/The Stock Market; b.r. Grant Heilman; Background photo by Scott Harvey for MMSD. 46: Photo courtesy of Al Cetta. 78-79: Scott Harvey for MMSD. 80-81: Earl Ripling. 114: Courtesy of Bradbury Press. 115: Courtesy of Ashton Scholastic. 116: Courtesy of Jan Ormerod.

Macmillan/McGraw-Hill School Division
10 Union Square East
New York, New York 10003

Printed in the United States of America
ISBN 0-02-178753-0 / 1, L.3
3 4 5 6 7 8 9 RRW 99 98 97 96 95 94 93

CONTENTS

Higglety, Pigglety, Pop!

Higglety, pigglety, pop!
The dog has eaten the mop;
The pig's in a hurry,
The cat's in a flurry,
Higglety, pigglety, pop!

SAMUEL GOODRICH

9

Meet Taro Gomi

Taro Gomi lives in Japan. When he wrote *Coco Can't Wait!* he used Japanese words to tell the story. Later, the book was written in English, so more children could read it.

The author explains that in Japanese, Coco's name is Yo-chan. Yo-chan is also the name of his first daughter.

Taro Gomi was asked how he got the idea for this story. He said, "I knew a woman like Coco's grandmother. She would visit me without telling me she was coming."

Coco Can't Wait!

by
Taro
Gomi

Coco lives on top of the hill, in the house with the purple roof.

Grandma lives on the mountain, in the house with the orange roof.

One day Coco wanted to see
Grandma very much.

And Grandma wanted to see
Coco very much.

"Dear me! Coco is not here!"

"Oh no! Grandma is not here!"

"Oh no! Grandma is not here!"

"Dear me! Coco is not here!"

"I can't wait any longer."

"There isn't a minute to lose."

"Oh, how I want to see Grandma."

"Oh, how I want to see Coco."

"Hello, Grandma!"

"Hello, Coco!"

"Next time, Grandma, let's meet in
the middle, right under this tree."

And Grandma and Coco ate all the apples in Grandma's basket.

BY LAND

Trucks carry food
from farms to markets.

Cars travel across towns,
cities, and country roads.

HOW DO WE GET FROM

People go to work
by train.

Children go to school
on the school bus.

Amtrak

944

BY RAIL

BY SEA

Ships bring people and goods around the world.

HERE TO THERE?

People travel to all parts
of the world by jet.

A helicopter can land
almost anywhere.

BY AIR

43

THE FOLK WHO LIVE IN BACKWARD TOWN

The folk who live in Backward Town
Are inside out and upside down.
They wear their hats inside their heads
And go to sleep beneath their beds.
They only eat the apple peeling
And take their walks across the ceiling.

Mary Ann Hoberman

Meet Jeannette Caines

Jeannette Caines wrote *I Need a Lunch Box* after she heard about a little boy named Matthew who wanted a lunch box.

After she wrote the story, Ms. Caines found out that she wanted a lunch box, too! She says, "Lunch boxes are fun. When you don't have your lunch in them, you can put other things in them." Now Ms. Caines collects all different kinds of lunch boxes. She likes old ones best.

About books, Jeannette Caines says, "I read all the time. I carry a book wherever I go. I also carry paper and a pencil, in case I think of something to write. Reading and writing are wonderful."

Jeannette Caines

I NEED A LUNCH BOX

pictures by
Pat Cummings

My sister Doris got a brand new lunch box.
I need a lunch box too.
But Mommy said no lunch box until I start school.

Last week Daddy bought us new shoes.
Brown school shoes for Doris.
Black sneakers with yellow laces for me.

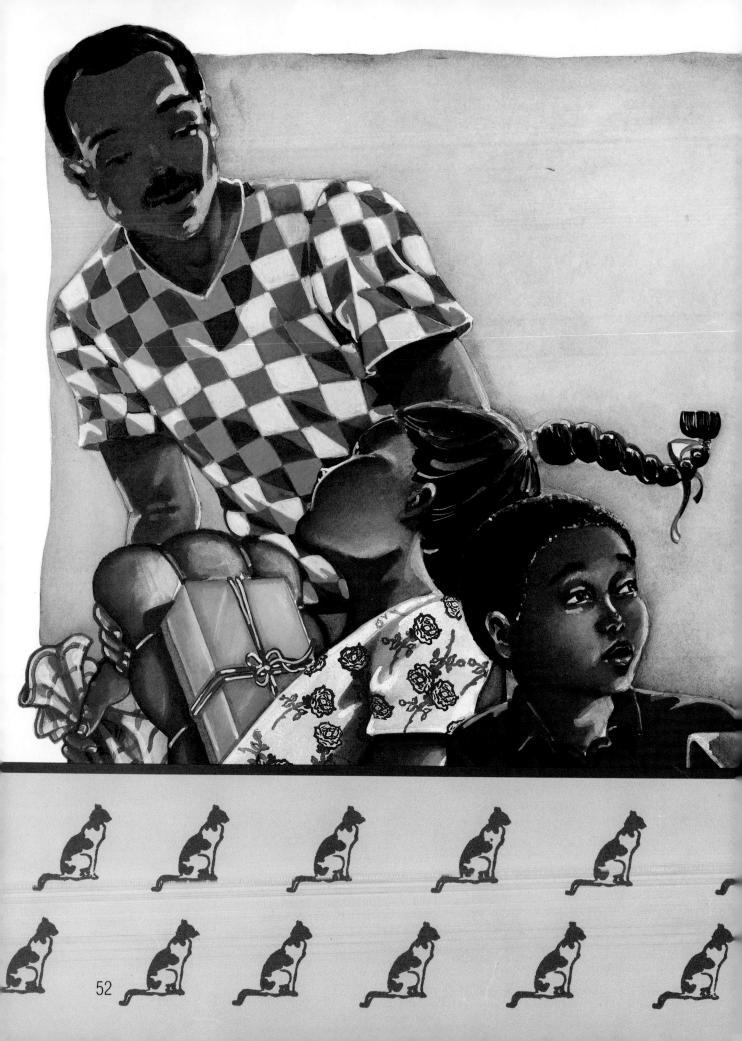

We walked past the lunch box counter, twice.
I need a lunch box!

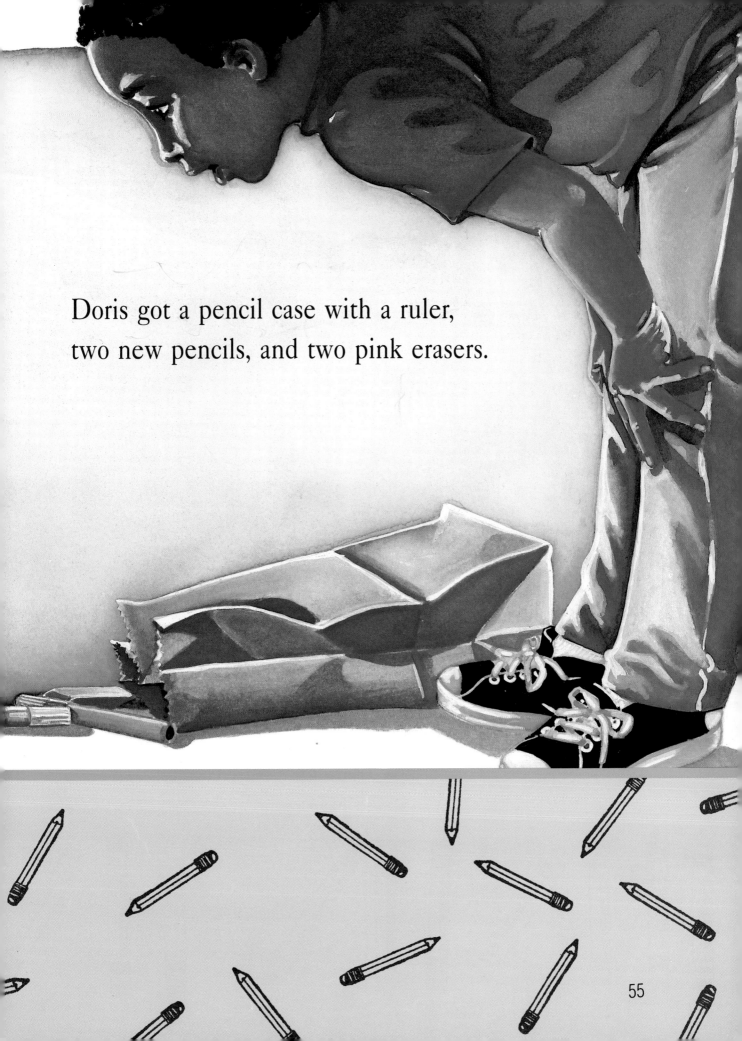

Doris got a pencil case with a ruler,
two new pencils, and two pink erasers.

All I got was a coloring book about space men and a box of crayons— but no lunch box.

Yesterday Doris got book covers, a raincoat, and an umbrella—all because she's going to first grade.

If I had a lunch box I could keep
my crayons in it. Or my marbles,
or bug collection, or toy animals.

I dreamed I had five lunch boxes, one for every day. Blue for Monday . . .

Green for Tuesday . . .

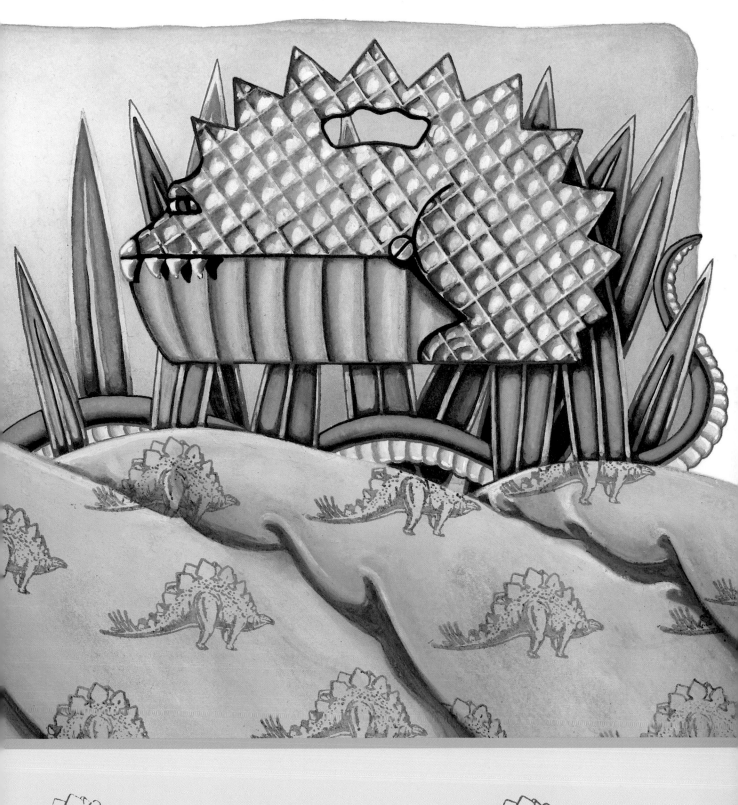

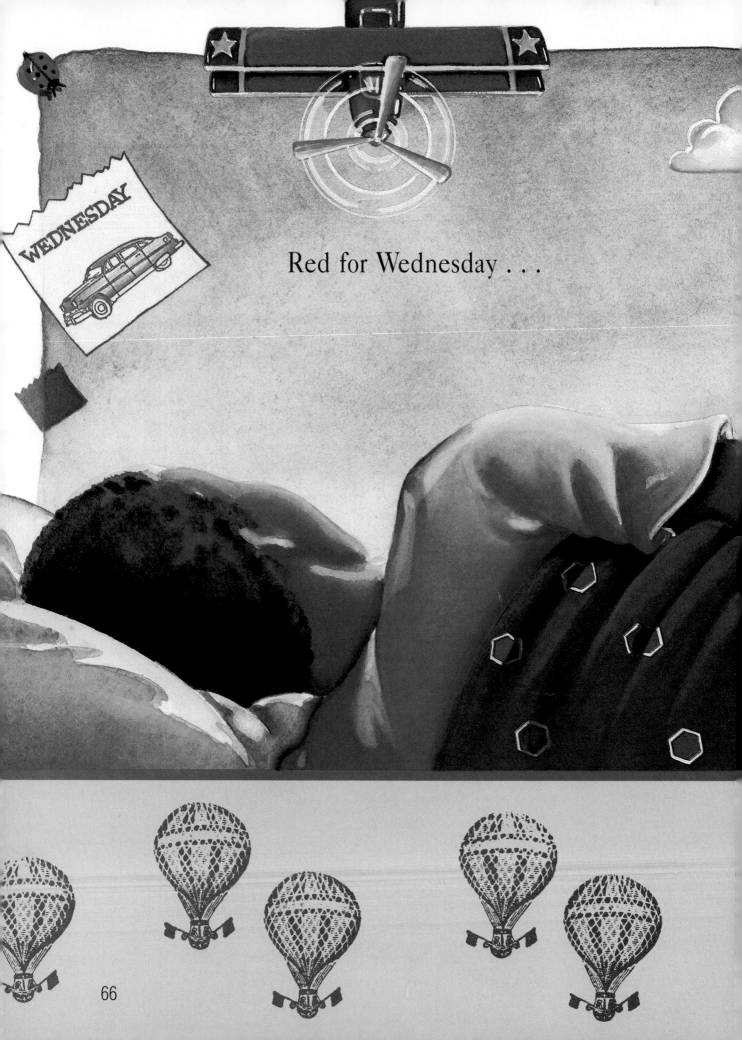

Red for Wednesday . . .

Purple for Thursday . . .

Yellow for Friday.

71

I filled them with peanut butter and jelly
sandwiches, apples, oranges, chocolate cake,
cookies and pies and donuts.
And then we had a lunch box parade.

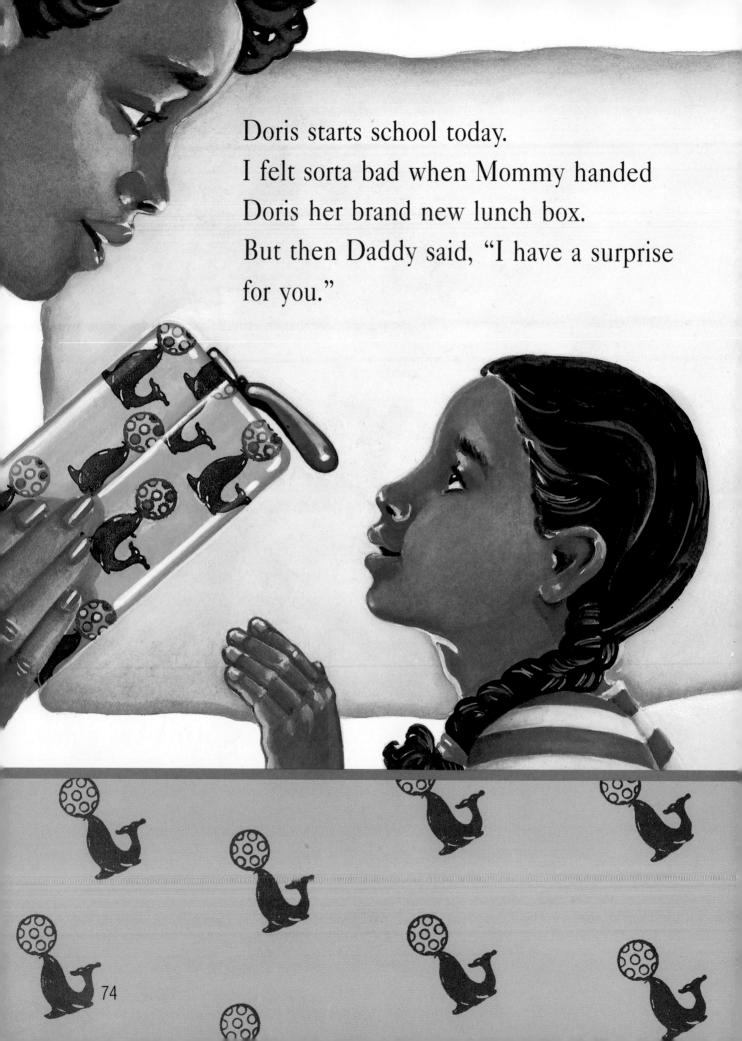

Doris starts school today.
I felt sorta bad when Mommy handed
Doris her brand new lunch box.
But then Daddy said, "I have a surprise
for you."

Wow!
I got a lunch box too!

Meet Pat Cummings

To make the pictures in *I Need a Lunch Box*, Pat Cummings used watercolor paints and rubber stamps. Artists use stamps when they want to use the same pictures over and over.

Ms. Cummings bought a few stamps, like the fish and dinosaurs, from a rubber-stamp man. But she couldn't find stamps for all the things she wanted. So she had her very own stamps made. "I drew pictures and a man made the stamps for me," she says.

"The funny thing was that he liked my stamps so much, he asked if he could make more of them to sell!"

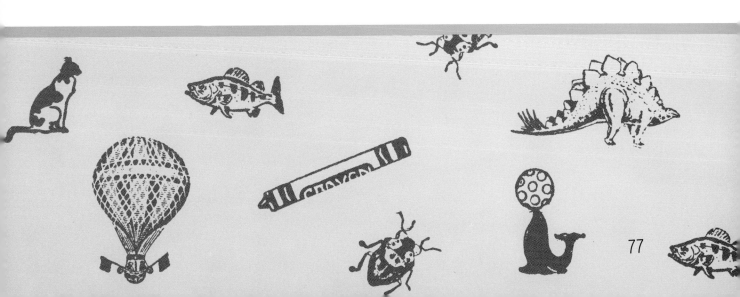

Robert,
Who Is Often a Stranger
to Himself

Do you ever look in the looking-glass

And see a stranger there?

A child you know and do not know,

Wearing what you wear?

Gwendolyn Brooks

79

SURPRISE!

The Surprise Party

Written and illustrated
by Pat Hutchins
Macmillan, 1986

"Rabbit is riding a flea tomorrow,"
whispered Mouse. "It's a surprise."

Whose Footprints?

Written and illustrated
by Masayuki Yabuuchi
Philomel, 1985

Two webbed footprints.
Whose are they?

Hattie
and the
Fox

Written by Mem Fox
Illustrated by Patricia Mullins

Hattie was a big black hen.
One morning she looked up and said,
"Goodness gracious me!
I can see a nose in the bushes!"

"Good grief!" said the goose.
"Well, well!" said the pig.

"Who cares?" said the sheep.
"So what?" said the horse.
"What next?" said the cow.

And Hattie said,
"Goodness gracious me!
I can see a nose
and two eyes in the bushes!"

"Good grief!" said the goose.
"Well, well!" said the pig.
"Who cares?" said the sheep.
"So what?" said the horse.
"What next?" said the cow.

And Hattie said,
"Goodness gracious me!
I can see a nose, two eyes,
and two ears in the bushes!"

"Good grief!" said the goose.
"Well, well!" said the pig.
"Who cares?" said the sheep.
"So what?" said the horse.
"What next?" said the cow.

And Hattie said,
"Goodness gracious me!
I can see a nose, two eyes, two ears,
and two legs in the bushes!"

"Good grief!" said the goose.
"Well, well!" said the pig.
"Who cares?" said the sheep.
"So what?" said the horse.
"What next?" said the cow.

And Hattie said,
"Goodness gracious me!
I can see a nose, two eyes, two ears, two legs,
and a body in the bushes!"

"Good grief!" said the goose.
"Well, well!" said the pig.
"Who cares?" said the sheep.
"So what?" said the horse.
"What next?" said the cow.

And Hattie said,
"Goodness gracious me!
I can see a nose, two eyes, two ears, a body, four legs,
and a tail in the bushes!
It's a fox! It's a fox!"
And she flew very quickly into a nearby tree.

"Oh, no!" said the goose.
"Dear me!" said the pig.
"Oh, dear!" said the sheep.
"Oh, help!" said the horse.

But the cow said, "MOO!"

so loudly that the fox was frightened and ran away.

And they were all so surprised
that none of them said anything
for a very long time.

Meet Mem Fox

When Mem Fox visits schools, she often invites children to read *Hattie and the Fox* aloud with her. She says it's lots of fun to say the words fast and then to say what the cow says in a very slow, deep voice.

Ms. Fox likes this story for other reasons, too. "There are many old stories about hens and foxes," she says. "But this one is new."

Mem Fox loves to read and write. She says, "Reading is the best way to learn how to write. Reading written words and hearing written words have taught me to write well."

Meet Patricia Mullins

To make the pictures for *Hattie and the Fox,* Patricia Mullins visited a special farm in the middle of a city. She went there every day to look at the animals and make drawings of them. "I always start my pictures by drawing live animals," she says. "I watch how they move. That helps me make them look more real in my pictures."

Later, Ms. Mullins tore pieces of colored tissue paper to look like the animals. Then she glued them down. Last, she used a crayon to draw a few lines. This way of making pictures is called collage.

Meet

JAN ORMEROD

Jan Ormerod was a child in Australia when she first heard *The Story of Chicken Licken*. "In some other countries, Chicken Licken is called Chicken Little," she says.

She thought it would be fun to have this book tell two stories. "The words tell about Chicken Licken," she says. "The pictures tell another story."

At the time Ms. Ormerod wrote this story, she had a baby that crawled everywhere. "I know the trouble a crawling baby can get into," she says.

Since Ms. Ormerod wrote this book, many school-children have invited her to see their own plays and puppet shows using the Chicken Licken story.

by
Jan
Ormerod

THE STORY OF
CHICKEN
LICKEN

OH, DUCK LUCK, DON'T GO!
I was going and I met Henny Penny,
and Henny Penny met Chicken Licken
and the sky had fallen
on her poor little head.
   Now we are going to tell the king.

OH, DRAKE LAKE, DON'T GO!
I was going and I met Cock Lock,
and Cock Lock met Henny Penny,
and Henny Penny met Chicken Licken
and the sky had fallen
    on her poor little head.
        Now we are going to tell the king.

OH, GOOSE LOOSE, DON'T GO!
I was going and I met Duck Luck,
and Duck Luck met Cock Lock,
and Cock Lock met Henny Penny,
and Henny Penny met Chicken Licken
and the sky had fallen
on her poor little head.
Now we are going to tell the king.

OH, GANDER LANDER, DON'T GO!
I was going and I met Drake Lake,
and Drake Lake met Duck Luck,
and Duck Luck met Cock Lock,
and Cock Lock met Henny Penny,
and Henny Penny met Chicken Licken
and the sky had fallen
on her poor little head.
Now we are going to tell the king.

So Gander Lander turned back and met Turkey Lurkey. He asked Turkey Lurkey where he was going.

I am going to the woods for some food.

OH, TURKEY LURKEY, DON'T GO!
I was going and I met Goose Loose,
and Goose Loose met Drake Lake,
and Drake Lake met Duck Luck,
and Duck Luck met Cock Lock,
and Cock Lock met Henny Penny,
and Henny Penny met
Chicken Licken and the sky
had fallen on her poor little head.
Now we are going to tell the king.

So Turkey Lurkey turned back and walked with Gander Lander, Goose Loose, Drake Lake, Duck Luck, Cock Lock, Henny Penny and Chicken Licken. As they were going along they met Foxy Woxy.

Where are you going?

Foxy Woxy took them
into the fox's hole.
He and his young ones
soon ate up poor Chicken Licken,
Henny Penny, Cock Lock, Duck Luck,
Drake Lake, Goose Loose,
Gander Lander and Turkey Lurkey.
So they never saw the king
and they never told him
that the sky had fallen.

Something  Has Been Here

Something big has been here,
what it was, I do not know,
for I did not see it coming,
and I did not see it go,
but I hope I never meet it,
if I do, I'm in a fix,
for it left behind its footprints,
they are size nine-fifty-six.

Jack Prelutsky